21<sup>st</sup> Century Junior Library

# FARM ANIMALS
# DOGS

by Cecilia Minden

CHERRY LAKE PUBLISHING * ANN ARBOR, MICHIGAN

Published in the United States of America by Cherry Lake Publishing
Ann Arbor, Michigan
www.cherrylakepublishing.com

Content Adviser: Laurie Rincker, Assistant Professor of Agriculture, Eastern Kentucky University

Photo Credits: Cover and page 4, ©Shawn Hine, used under license from Shutterstock, Inc.; cover and page 6, ©Nicolay Titov, used under license from Shutterstock, Inc.; page 8, ©Jeff Greenberg/Alamy; cover and page 10, ©Dizajune/Dreamstime.com; cover and page 12, ©Ankevanwyk/Dreamstime.com; page 14, ©iStockphoto.com/EEI_Tony; page 16, ©jeff gynane, used under license from Shutterstock, Inc.; page 18, ©Pretorius/Dreamstime.com; page 20, ©Assorted Imagery By Phil/Alamy

**LIBRARY OF CONGRESS CATALOGING-IN-PUBLICATION DATA**
Minden, Cecilia.
  Farm animals. Dogs / by Cecilia Minden.
     p. cm.—(21st century junior library)
  Includes bibliographical references and index.
  ISBN-13: 978-1-60279-547-1
  ISBN-10: 1-60279-547-9
  1. Dogs—Juvenile literature. I. Title. II. Title: Dogs. III. Series.
  SF426.5.M57 2009
  636.7—dc22                                               2009005034

*Cherry Lake Publishing would like to acknowledge the work of
The Partnership for 21st Century Skills.
Please visit www.21stcenturyskills.org for more information.*

# CONTENTS

Farm dogs come in all shapes and sizes.

# Who Says Woof?

Think of different farm animals. You might picture chickens, goats, and cows. Did you know that dogs are important farm animals, too?

Dogs make great pets. Dogs may also have special jobs. Some of these dogs live on farms. Different **breeds** of dogs are trained for farm jobs. Let's learn more about farm dogs.

There can be several puppies in a litter.

# Puppy Love

**B**aby dogs are called **pups** or puppies. Pups are born in a **litter**. They cannot see or hear for the first 10 days. Puppies need their mother to feed them. They drink milk from their mother. Pups drink milk until they are about 6 weeks old. Then they are **weaned** to solid food.

Choosing the right dog is important. It might not be easy.

How do farmers pick the perfect dog for the farm? They pay attention to many things when making their choice.

They watch all of the pups carefully. They don't want to choose a shy puppy. They prefer one that is friendly. It should also be independent. A good farm dog isn't one that needs a lot of attention.

Farm dogs need to be comfortable around other farm animals.

Farmers will choose a pup that does not fight with its brothers and sisters. They want a dog that will not be bothered by other animals.

The farmer may make a loud noise around the pup. Does the pup check it out or hide? A good farm dog is not afraid to explore.

**Think!**

Some pups always want people to pet them. They may not make good farm dogs. Think about dogs that always want attention. How might that keep them from doing their jobs well? Hint: Would these dogs like to be on their own?

A good farm dog should follow a
farmer's commands.

# Life on the Farm

**A** farm dog needs special training. The new dog is trained to sit, wait, and come. Some farmers pair the dog with another young animal. Lambs are one choice. Why might young farm dogs be put with another animal? This helps the dog get used to being around **livestock**.

Coyotes will kill farm animals for food. Dogs help protect herds from coyotes and other predators.

Farmers also train dogs to bark at the right time. The dogs are checked each time they bark. They are rewarded for barking if another animal is in danger. Dogs are taught to bark only if there is a problem.

Dogs learn to bark as a warning to farmers. Farmers have to be patient while the dogs learn.

Some dogs herd geese.

How else are dogs trained? It depends on what the farmer needs. Some dogs are taught to **herd** sheep and goats. Others become guard dogs for young animals or the **henhouse**.

**Ask Questions!**

Do you know someone who owns a dog? Ask that person why he chose the dog he did. Find out how he trained the dog. Asking questions is a good way to learn more about dogs.

Dog breeds often have a specific purpose.
Australian cattle dogs are used to herd cattle.

# Showing Off

Border collies and shepherds are two kinds of good farm dogs. The best dog is sometimes a mix of many breeds.

Farm dogs are smart. They work very hard, too. They are an important part of the farm family.

This border collie is herding sheep in a contest.

It can be fun to watch farm dogs do their jobs. Check your local area for dog shows. Dogs herd livestock during some of these shows. See for yourself the amazing things farm dogs can do!

**Create!**

Farm dogs use their **senses** to do their jobs. Draw a picture of a dog. Label the parts of the dog's body used to see, hear, smell, and taste things. How do you think dogs use their senses to keep other farm animals safe?

# GLOSSARY

**breeds** (BREEDZ) specific types or kinds of animals

**henhouse** (HEN-houss) a house for chickens

**herd** (HURD) to make animals move together as a group

**litter** (LIT-ur) a group of certain baby animals born to the same mother at the same time

**livestock** (LIVE-stok) animals raised on a farm or ranch

**pups** (PUHPSS) young dogs

**senses** (SENSS-iz) ways in which living things learn about their surroundings such as by seeing and hearing

**weaned** (WEEND) switched to eating solid foods instead of drinking milk from an animal's mother

22

# FIND OUT MORE

## BOOKS

Endres, Hollie. *Dogs*. Minneapolis: Bellwether Media, 2008.

Walker, Kathryn. *See How Dogs Grow*. New York: Rosen Publishing Group's PowerKids Press, 2009.

## WEB SITES

### Animal Planet—Breed All About It: Border Collie
*animal.discovery.com/videos/breed-all-about-it-border-collie.html*
Watch a short video of Border Collies in action

### KidsHealth—Dogs and Preventing Dog Bites
*kidshealth.org/kid/watch/out/dogs.html*
Learn ways to stay safe around dogs

# INDEX

## ABOUT THE AUTHOR

Cecilia Minden, PhD, is a literacy consultant and author of many books for children. She lives with her family near Chapel Hill, North Carolina. The four-footed member of Cecilia's family is a much-loved Yorkie named Kenzie.

ML

S/
/
/